Taking the Words off the Wall

How to Create and Use Word Walls

Libby Larrabee

Kathie Heap

DOMINIE PRESS

Pearson Learning Group

Dedicated to my dad for his never-ending interest and encouragement, and especially my husband, Dick, for supporting me in all I do. – LL

This book is dedicated to the circle of women who continue to support me, my five sisters, and in memory of my mother, Grace Piette. – KH

Acknowledgments

The authors would like to thank the many colleagues who shared their teaching and tried new techniques as we wrote, especially Jane Cutler from Ezra Baker Elementary and the Word Wall Wizards at Moreland Hills Elementary. Laura Schaaf and her teachers shared the "Instructional Continuum for Learning Words in Small Groups."

Our special thanks goes to Sarah Johnson, who carefully read and edited our manuscript.

Our publisher, Raymond Yuen, and the staff at Dominie Press are always ready with support and suggestions. It is an honor to work with them.

Publisher: Raymond Yuen
Consultant: Dr. Adria F. Klein
Editor: Bob Rowland
Designer: Natalie Chupil

ISBN 0-7685-0624-7
Printed in Singapore by PH Productions Pte Ltd
3 4 5 6 PH 09 08 07 06 05

Pearson Learning Group

1-800-321-3106
www.pearsonlearning.com

Table of Contents

Why a Word Wall?

What is a word wall?

Why should I have one in my classroom?

Will it really help my students become better readers and writers?

How do I choose the words that go up on the wall?

Can I buy a word wall?

You may have asked these questions when you picked up this book. A word wall is a systematically organized collection of words displayed in large letters on a wall or other large display place in the classroom (Cunningham 1995). Patricia Cunningham and Richard Allington recommended the word wall as a teaching tool for vocabulary instruction in their book *Classrooms That Work* (1994). The concept was developed further in Cunningham's *Phonics They Use* (1995). Originally designed to help students learn the common words they need to read and write, word walls now also serve as reference tools for students as they learn about how words work. Over time, a word wall takes on a life of its own. We see it as an evolving tool that is constructed by teachers and children to facilitate reading and writing instruction. While much has been written about this teaching tool, and pre-made word walls are now available for purchase, word walls are not effective unless teachers see the big picture of how they fit into a comprehensive literacy approach. The principles of teaching and learning in an effective literacy approach are based on:

- modeled teacher demonstrations
- guided practice
- learner independence

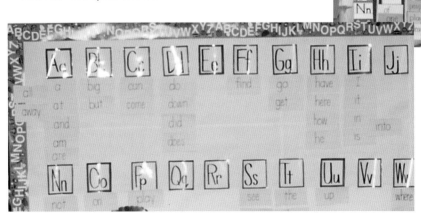

As teachers work with word walls, they move through a continuum of understanding about the purpose of a word wall and how it works. Their progression often looks like this:

A word wall is put up in its entirety because everyone else has one, or because it is dictated by curriculum. It is not used as a daily teaching tool.

The initial word wall comes down. The teacher explains to the children how it works and what it's for and engages the children in the process of constructing a word wall that is to be used as a resource.

Both the teacher and the students construct the word wall. It becomes an integral part of literacy learning and is referred to and referenced throughout each day.

The teacher develops an awareness that ongoing assessment around the word wall needs to happen in the following areas:
• word wall checks
• records of oral text reading
• unedited rough drafts in writing

The teacher uses assessment information to teach children how to independently take words apart while reading and constructing words in their writing.

In this book we strive to help you not only understand the "big picture," but also learn how to look at student reading and writing samples to make decisions about what should and should not be put up on the wall throughout the school year as students move toward independence. We include snippets from records of oral reading and writing samples to help you assess what children are learning about words and how they work.

In their book, *Word Matters* (1998), Fountas and Pinnell discuss word walls as a way to support the teaching of important general principles about words and how they work.

- Word walls are a reference tool that can be used by students as they learn to become independent readers and writers.
- Word walls are a visual reinforcement of the connections and characteristics that help children learn about words and how they work.
- Word walls represent not only words the children are in the process of learning, but exemplars of word principles that have been introduced in whole group mini-lessons.

Explicit examples of mini-lessons are featured in Chapter 4.

Ultimately, everything you are doing in connection with the word wall leads to one goal:

Students at some point will need to internalize the process of how words work, making connections and using analogies in order to effectively and efficiently take words apart in reading and construct words in writing without teacher support.

Children who have successfully learned how to read and write independently are able to do all of this in a fast, flexible, and fluent way with very little conscious attention to the process.

This book aims to demonstrate to teachers that all the activities, demonstrations, and teaching that focus on the word wall are in service of this goal.

The keys to a successful word wall, one that students will use and learn from, are:
- Choosing words that children need to know in reading and writing, and being selective about the choices.
- Placing the word wall where the children can see it easily. It should be a focal point in the room.
- Introducing the words gradually (no more than five a week) and in a way that children will want to know them.
- Practicing with the words on the wall daily and making it fun.
- Referring to the wall in a variety of teaching situations throughout the day so that children will refer to it themselves independently.
- Actively demonstrating how the words on the wall are useful to students in reading and writing.

In the following chapters, you will learn about the most powerful and effective ways to incorporate word walls into a comprehensive literacy program.

2 Whose Wall Is It, Anyway?

*"I've put a word wall up in my room, and none
of my students use it or even look at it."*

*"I've had a word wall hanging up in the room all year
and they STILL ask me how to spell words."*

*"I constructed a word wall before school started,
but I can't say that I've done much with it."*

*"I've noticed word walls in many classrooms in my
school, so I put one up, too. Now, what do I DO with it?"*

*"I took my word wall down because my student teacher needed a place to put
her bulletin board on the environment. Is that OK? The kids weren't using it, anyway."*

These are some of the comments we hear over and over as we work in schools with teachers in their classrooms. Many teachers are aware that word walls can be used as an effective teaching tool, but they don't fully understand their purpose or how to introduce and work with them powerfully throughout the year.

There are two important factors to consider before a word wall can ever become a successful teaching tool:
1. Teachers need to develop a theoretical and practical understanding of the purpose of the word wall and how it works.
2. Children need to be involved in the ongoing construction of the word wall.

Teachers who have explored word walls over time have realized that their construction will vary from year to year, depending on the strengths and needs of each class. Although common lists of high frequency words (such as Fry or Dolch) can be used as a reference, there need not be any prescribed, sequential order as to which words go up when.

Our goal is that you will gain that theoretical and practical understanding and be able to use this teaching tool in fun, constructive ways to support your students' word learning in reading and writing.

The word wall allows teachers to have an ongoing, functional record of what has been explicitly taught in a mini-lesson involving the whole class. This teaching focuses primarily on words frequently encountered in reading and writing (for example, *to*, *it*, and *me*) and words that contain parts, or clusters of letters, that can be used to problem solve an unknown word (for example, using <u>just</u> to get to bl<u>ust</u>ery). The research of Goswami and Bryant (1990) demonstrates that children can learn to use their understanding of words and word parts to write and read words that are new to them. All children have the ability to use word parts and analogies, once they have been taught how.

The word wall serves as a mediator, a concrete resource that is adjusted over time as children move:

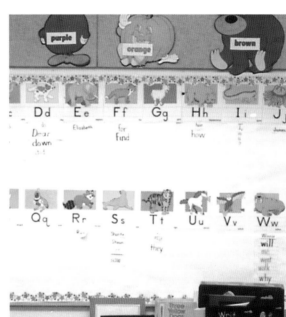

- from the demonstration given by the teacher
- into guided practice in a variety of settings
- to independent use in reading and writing tasks.

A word wall needs to be co-constructed by the class and the teacher, using words the children need to know for the material they are currently reading and writing. The word wall serves as a support and a tool that enables children to learn new words and how to use these known words to get to the unknown words that they need to read and write.

When teachers understand the value of word walls in word learning, the word wall can evolve into a classroom resource that children use daily and perceive as valuable to their learning. Children must be engaged in the process of constructing the word wall and encouraged to use it through a variety of activities. The teacher, who involves the children and refers to the wall and its function daily, will find that children use it over and over again in their reading and writing.

If the students are not aware of how a word wall will help to make their reading and writing easier, then constructing one will be a waste of time. Engaging children in the construction of the word wall is key.

Much has been written about the level of engagement and investment that must exist within all learners.

It is a teacher's responsibility, not the pupil's, to make sure that *what* children are expected to learn has the possibility of making sense, not only in terms of what the children know already, but also in terms of what they might want to know (Smith 1997, p. 81).

This is how the word wall helps me. I can look at the word wall if I am reading and I don't know a word. If I am writing and I can't spell a word, I can look at the word wall. If I need to spell a word like popped, I could look for the word stopped.

Molly – Grade 3

The word wall helps me with a lot of things like spelling. If I write a paragraph I sometimes have trouble with spelling. Sometimes the word wall gives me ideas about what to write, and when I write a poem it helps me with rhyme.

Katy – Grade 3

The word wall helps me to spell, and it helps me not to forget the i in believe and the double p in stopped.

Daniel – Grade 3

Engagement occurs when students are convinced:
- They are capable of learning and doing what is being demonstrated.
- They believe that the learning has value, purpose, and use for them.
- They are free from anxiety.
- They admire, like, respect, and trust the teacher (Cambourne 1988, p. 21).

Because the word wall is such a valuable tool for students to use while constructing words in writing and breaking down words in reading, a teacher who understands its purpose will actively involve the students in its daily use and will model, guide, and support the students' ever-increasing independent use of the wall.

The Names Chart

A precursor to the word wall in kindergarten and first grade is the Names Chart. The children's names are grouped alphabetically. Initially, first names of the children are used, but after awhile last names and other names can be added. A large piece of tagboard or poster board works well for this chart. Leave room to add the names of new students who enter during the year. In classrooms with a high transiency rate, using Velcro backing on the names can make rearranging them easier.

It is important to create the Names Chart with the children and then actively refer to it in your daily shared and interactive reading and writing experiences.
- In shared reading, when you are reading a text that is visible to the class, highlight a word and ask whose name on the Names Chart begins (or ends or has a part) like that word.
- In interactive writing, when you are co-constructing a text with the class, ask the children to search the Names Chart to start to write a word (or write a part of a word).

When you actively incorporate work with the Names Chart in your daily reading and writing, you are beginning to help children learn how to:

- Look at words and word parts in more detail. A Names Chart is a great tool for teaching sound-to-letter correspondence.
- Use what they know to get to something new. A Names Chart is a record of some known information for each child in the room.
- Use a reference tool in the classroom independently.

Words We Know Chart

Another chart that is especially helpful in kindergarten before introducing a word wall is the Words We Know Chart. This chart is a listing of the high utility words that children are beginning to learn. Words on this chart might include *I, see, can, to, etc.*

You might begin the chart by talking about a word in a shared reading experience and then writing it on the chart. Later, you can refer to the chart when writing the word in your interactive writing session. The chart will grow as more words are highlighted and used in reading and writing experiences. You may decide at some time during the year that the chart is getting too full (12-15 words) and the children understand the basic purpose of such a list. This is the time to begin constructing the word wall with the children.

Words We Know

I

can

see

the

like

and

me

look

is

3 Setting up a Word Wall

"Where will I put it?"
A word wall needs to be placed where there is a clear, unobstructed view from all areas of the classroom. A blank bulletin board or wall is perfect, but not every classroom has the ideal spot. Be creative! We have seen word walls on window shades and even on a clear shower curtain draped across several windows. You may even have to give up your favorite chalkboard or whiteboard! Just make sure the word wall is at the children's eye level and can be easily read. The spaces above or below the chalkboard are not always good spots, but this, too, varies in each classroom.

"What should I use for the background and the word cards?"
We suggest having a solid colored, dark background for your word wall (unless you use the shower curtain idea over your windows) so that the word cards will stand out and be easily read.

Card stock about the width of a sentence strip (3 inches) will provide a sturdy card. You do not need to cut the cards the same length. Each card should be just long enough for the word. It is not necessary to show the configuration of the word. There is no definitive research that shows that this makes learning the words on the wall any easier. Make the print on the cards as large as possible. Have the words laminated after you introduce them, if you can, because chances are good that you will use many of them in the years to come.

Write the words on the cards with a black broad-tip marker. White or cream-colored cards are good for non-generative, high frequency words such as *I, was,* and *the.* Use pale-colored cards for generative words such as *can, like,* and *play.* Generative words or exemplars are words that contain key word features or patterns that children can use to form many other words (for example, knowing *play* will help them know *away*). When generative words are written on pale-colored cards, the children can quickly locate those words that will help them read and write new and unfamiliar words.

You also will need to think about the header letter cards you will use and how you will attach the cards to the wall. These letter cards are placed alphabetically on the word wall and spaced so that words beginning with that letter can go underneath. Many teachers simply put up cards that have the upper and lower case letter. This is certainly appropriate for the upper primary grades. You may, however, wish to add a key picture for each letter on the header cards.

This is especially helpful in kindergarten and first grade. If you do, make sure the picture is consistent with your ABC chart and any individual alphabet charts the children may have pasted in their writing journals.

Some thought needs to be given to attaching the cards. We believe children need to be able to "take the words off the wall," literally and figuratively. Many teachers use Velcro so that words can be moved around as more are added under a given letter.

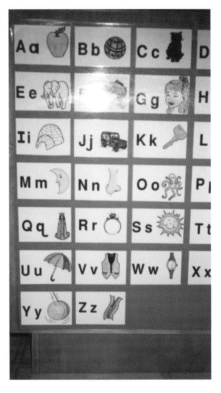

As high utility words become known by all of the children, talk to them about removing some of them and storing them elsewhere. We have also found it helpful to have a duplicate set of the word cards for student use. These duplicate cards can be available for practice activities and center activities. A variety of these activities can be found in Chapter 3.

Following are some ways to store these cards:
- A ring of cards for each letter hung at the bottom of your word wall.
- A file box of words.
- A library pocket for each letter placed along the bottom of the word wall.

Overall, the word wall should have an organized look so that it will be a resource that is easy for you and the children to use throughout each day.

"How Do I Start?"

Now that you have found the best place in your classroom for the word wall and have prepared the header cards and background, you are ready to think about how you will introduce the word wall to the children and how you will select the first words to go on it.

If you teach kindergarten, you should wait until there are a good number of words on your Words We Know Chart before beginning a word wall. You might begin a word wall halfway through the year, or, if it seems appropriate, toward the end of the year. It depends on your individual class and the number of words your students seem to be able to handle.

Some time during the school year, kindergarten teachers start a word wall by referring to the Words We Know Chart and the number of words on it. Dialogue for introducing a word wall might be:

> *Boys and girls, you have learned how to read and write so many new words that our Words We Know Chart is getting full. Today we are going write the words we know on cards and put them on this word wall under the letter they start with. All the words we are learning will go up here under the letter they begin with. That way, when you are writing and when you are reading you can check the word wall to help you think about the word you are working on. Let's start by putting your names up there.*

You would then pass out children's name cards ready to be put on the wall. The children would take turns putting their names under the appropriate letter on the wall.

First and second grade teachers will want to take stock of the words the children know already. Check with the previous year's teachers to see what words they had on their word wall. What words did the children manage to learn? Finding out about the words the children were working with during the previous year will give you a good idea of where to begin. You will want to find out:
• Which words were removed from the wall after the children easily learned them.
• Which words the children seemed to use frequently.
• Which words the children struggled with.

To find out which words the children remember, give some type of assessment at the beginning of the year. Select 10 to 20 words that are common to the past year's word walls, dictate them to the children, and have them write the words. If the majority of your class is able to write the words correctly, then all of those words don't need to go on the word wall. For the small percentage of children who have not yet learned those words, we suggest an individual word wall in a manila folder.

If your class has not had any experience with word walls, look at a list of words most frequently encountered in text at your grade level. Common word lists such as Fry and Dolch can be used as a reference.

Choose a few of the words known by all the children to put on the word wall. By starting with some known words, you enable the children to begin using the word wall immediately.

Once evidence of known words is established, teachers in first and second grade might introduce their word walls with dialogue like this:

> *Today we are going to start our word wall and put up some words that you know from last year. Let's talk about some of the words you learned in kindergarten (or first grade). Can anyone think of a word wall word you learned how to read and write last year? Let's write the words on this chart. Great, this is a good start.*

Choose a few of the words to begin your word wall work.

"How Do I Choose New Words to Go on the Wall?"
The biggest challenge for teachers is deciding which new words to introduce as the year progresses. There are many word lists to choose from, and your school district may have adopted a list of words that have to be learned at each grade level. Some authors suggest many different kinds of word walls. We suggest that the focus of your word wall should be on:
• high utility words that children use daily in their reading and writing, and
• generative words that will help children use known words to get to new words.

Other words such as science words, math words, and theme-related words should be placed on different word charts. Specialty words such as compound words and homophones can also be placed on other charts with one or two exemplars that might be difficult (such as *there*, *their*, *they're*) placed on the word wall.

High Utility Words

What are the high utility words children need to know in order to read and write at your grade level? If you have a reading series, look at the words suggested as vocabulary to be learned and then "*pare down the list.*" Choose words that are frequently encountered in text, but don't select a word like *sister* just because it is in the story. Will the reader be able to predict the word from context in the story or get to it through sound analysis? If so, then it probably isn't a good high utility word for your wall word.

Early readers predict text based on their background knowledge and their knowledge of language structure. When they can identify even a few high utility words in text, those words serve as "islands of certainty" (Clay, 1991 p.172) and help them learn to monitor or check their reading using visual information.

In kindergarten and early first grade, look for the high utility words that appear in the big books you are using during shared reading. Look at the interactive writing pieces you have collaborated on. What are the words that pop up over and over? These will be good words for the word wall.

Later in first grade and into second grade, let the books the children are reading and the words they are struggling with in their writing be your guide in choosing the most needed words for the wall. What are the words the children are using in their writing that they have difficulty spelling? Are there words that the children ask you to spell repeatedly? Take a look at the following writing samples to see what words might be chosen.

The first word list below is from a publisher's anthology; the list on the right features the words we would consider putting on the word wall as high utility words.

asked	some
flour	these
found	who
help	
into	
plant	
some	
these	
who	

Although into *is a word frequently used, we wouldn't choose it, because the words* in *and* to *would be words already on the wall.*

In this writing sample we might choose:
went, put, find

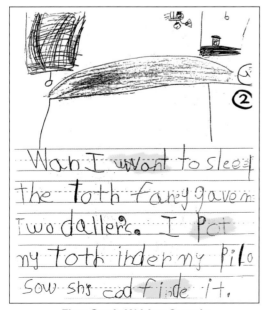

First Grade Writing Sample

In this writing sample we might choose:
went, took, there, were

Second Grade Writing Sample

Here are some sample pages from books across emergent, early, and fluent readers in first and second grade. We have identified one or two words we might choose. What are some words you would choose?

In this text we might choose: *said* and *who.*

Helping, by Joy Cowley
(Published by Dominie Press)
Emergent Level

In this text we might choose: *hurry* and *work.*

One Sock, Two Socks, by Judy Owens
(Published by Dominie Press)
Early Level

In this text we might choose: *type* and *raise.*

Habitats of the World: Polar Regions,
by Alison Ballance
(Published by Dominie Press)
Fluent Level

Generative Words

Generative words, or exemplars, are words containing key word features or patterns that children can use to form other words. When taught, children can use this type of word as an analogy to help them read and write words that are unfamiliar.

> *Generating words is not about building word families. It is producing a word you need to write by any means at your disposal and getting as close as you can to the way it is probably written in English. For that kind of problem solving a rich collection of known words will be invaluable (Clay 2001, p. 24).*

Before children can begin to learn about making analogies, they have to begin to build this rich collection of words. It is equally important that they have learned "how to" learn a word. It's not about amassing known words, but more about developing the ability to look at a word and remember the unique visual features that set it apart from other known words. (Suggestions for helping children learn how to do this are found in Chapter 5.)

Teachers can begin to help children learn to look at words in a variety of ways for problem solving by first helping them use the concept of changing the onset to make new words. The onset consists of the consonant/s that come before the vowel in a syllable or single-syllable word. The rime is the vowel and the consonants that come after the vowel.

Onset	Rime
c	an
pl	ay

Once children begin to understand how to use analogy to get from a known word to a new word, you should begin to teach and explore the different word principles with your students. This kind of work will continue to help your students build a flexible way of looking at words that they need to problem-solve. As you teach these principles, exemplars of the principle are added to the word wall.

Wylie and Durrell's (1970) list of common rimes would be a good place to begin to help children learn how to use analogy. More than 500 words can be made with these 37 rimes.

ack	ail	ain	ake	ale
ame	an	ank	ap	ash
at	ate	aw	ay	eat
ell	est	ice	ick	ide
ight	ill	in	ine	ing
ink	ip	it	ock	oke
op	ore	ot	uck	ug
ump	unk			

The next level of challenge would be rimes with more silent letters that require an increased ability to notice visual features of spelling patterns and an awareness of the variant sounds of certain rimes. Some of these rimes would include the following:

aught	ause	aight	atch	ange
eight	ealth	eive	ease	ise
ience	ieve	ield	ough	ous
other	ound	ought	ould	own

These word principles will be the focus of your mini-lessons. You will want to look at your students' records of text reading and writing samples to decide which principle needs to be taught next. Some examples follow.

Word Principles

Change the beginning
- Change the initial letter (_c_an, _m_an)
- Change letter clusters at the beginning (_pl_ay, _st_ay)
- Add letters to the beginning (and, _b_and)

Change the end
- Change the final letter (ca_n_, ca_t_)
- Add letters to the end to make new words (see , see_d_)
- Add endings (-s, -ed, -ing, -er, etc.)

Change the middle
- Change the letter in the middle (b_a_g, b_i_g, b_u_g)
- Change letter clusters in the middle (b_ar_n, b_ur_n, r_ea_d, r_ai_d)

Change the beginning and end at the same time
- Change letters at the beginning and end (_n_ee_d_, _s_ee_n_)
- Add letters at the beginning and end (an, _p_lan, _p_lan_ner_)

Words can be learned through analogy
- Known words can be used to solve a new word (no, go)
- Parts of words can be used to solve a new word (_st_op, _pl_ay, _st_ay)

Words can be put together to make new words
- in to → into

Some words sound the same and look different and have different meanings
- see, sea

Some words look the same and sound different and have different meanings
- read, read

Change the beginnings of words: Change the first letter.

In this first record of oral reading (see Appendix A, Page 51, for coding conventions), it is evident that the child has successfully learned to decode words by sounding them out phoneme by phoneme. While this is an important learning for the developing reader, good readers soon learn to look for and analyze larger chunks of visual information. Children with records of oral reading that look like this need to be taught the concept of onset and rime and how the first letter(s) can be changed to make new words. This would be an appropriate principle for this child to learn next.

√   w-e-n-t √   in- s-i-d √
Mom   went   inside,

√   √   b-a-ck√   √   √   √
and   came   back   with   a   bucket.

√   √   h-e-l-p √   √   √
"Come   and   help   me,   Nick,"

√   √   √   √   √
she   said.   "Here   we   go.

√   √   √   √   g-r-a-y- A
Look!   The   water   is   gray."   T

√   √   √   √   √   √
"Snowy   is   all   wet,"   said   Nick.

√   √
"Oh,   Snowy!"

Change the ending of words: Add endings.

In this writing sample, the child has not learned to use some of the common inflectional endings that children need to take on in their writing. Explicit instruction in adding endings such as *–ed* would be important for this child.

David	**puld**	**on**	**grey**	**slacs**	**and**	**a**	**sirt.**	**He**	**pict**	**up**	**a**
David	pulled	on	gray	slacks	and	a	shirt.	He	picked	up	a

pakig.	**He**	**cared**	**it**	**over**	**to**	**Brent**	**house**	**and**	**yelld**
package.	He	carried	it	over	to	Brent's	house	and	yelled

surprus.	**Brent**	**must**	**of**	**got**	**a**	**presint**	**that**	**he**	**alwaz**
surprise.	Brent	must	of	got	a	present	that	he	always

wantid	**and**	**he**	**said**	**thanks.**
wanted	and	he	said	thanks.

After teaching this principle to your students, put an exemplar of each word with the different sound of the -ed ending on the word wall (for example, *asked, played, wanted*).

Change the middle of words.

As children become more successful analyzing new words, you may notice that many of their substitutions have the same beginning and ending letters as the word in text. It is the middle of the word that they are not looking at carefully enough. Many times the substitution is still meaningful. Teaching children to change the middle letters in words will help focus their attention on all parts of an unfamiliar word. In this record of oral reading, you can see that the child is beginning to take another look, especially when meaning breaks down.

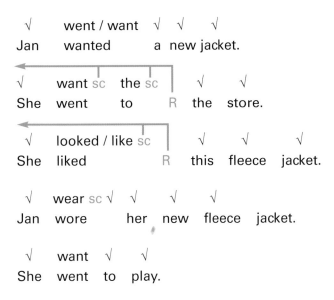

```
    √     went / want  √   √    √
  Jan     wanted       a  new  jacket.

  √     want sc  the sc  |  √     √
She     went     to      R  the   store.

  √     looked / like sc  |  √      √      √
She     liked              R  this  fleece  jacket.

  √     wear sc √  √     √      √
Jan     wore       her  new   fleece  jacket.

  √     want  √    √
She     went  to  play.
```

Ongoing analysis of your students' records of oral reading and writing will help you make decisions about the principles that will be most beneficial to teach. To maximize your instructional time, consider what is appropriate for your grade level and look at the number of children who are not yet successfully using that principle in their reading and writing.

4 Knowing the Words on the Wall

New words should be added weekly to the word wall throughout the year. Ongoing assessment of students' reading and writing will identify who is learning the words and who is still having difficulty. Whole group and small group instruction, as well as practice in refining concepts in a word study center, will facilitate this learning.

In this chapter we show you how this understanding can best be taught in the context of activities that occur in:
- Whole group mini-lessons to introduce new words.
- Ongoing assessment to assess who is learning the words.
- Whole class practice.
- Small groups for those not learning the words (teaching how to learn words).
- Heterogeneously grouped word study centers.

Whole Group Mini-lessons

Putting High Frequency Words on the Wall

Most teachers choose three to five new words to be introduced every week. Once you have reviewed your assessments and chosen the word or words you feel the children need to learn

next, gather them together near the word wall and have a conversation that *might* sound like the following examples:

Grade 1: Dialogue with the Class on Learning the Word "for"

Teacher:	I saw several of you read our new word, *for,* today in your books. (Names two children and tells them she saw them read the word *for.*)
Teacher:	(Puts the word wall card for the word on the easel.) Would we use this word to say, "I'm holding up four fingers," or, "I like to go to the grocery store for some milk"?
Children:	I like to go to the grocery store for some milk.
Teacher:	Let's snap the word *for.* (The children snap their fingers and say the letters *f-o-r.* Then they say the word.
Teacher:	Clap the word *for.*
Teacher:	Write the word on the carpet.
Teacher:	What is the tallest letter?
Child:	The letter *f.*
Teacher:	What does that letter look like to you?
Child:	A rainbow shape on top.
Teacher:	What do you notice about the way the word *for* looks?
Child:	One tall letter and two short letters.
Another Child:	Take the *f* off and it will say *or.*
Teacher:	Let's write this word *for.* (Models forming the letters in the word on the easel. Forms the letter *f* and describes formation in the same language as the school system's handwriting program. Uses the same language consistently throughout the lesson.)
Teacher:	Brings different children up to form the letters and then gets them to describe how to form each letter in the word while using consistent language. While the children are forming letters in the word, she says, "I like the way you made that *f* a tall letter."
Teacher:	Asks the class to evaluate how the children wrote various letters, stressing that they need to be started from the top down and that the letters *o* and *r* are the same height.
Teacher:	Where would you expect to find the word *for* on the word wall?

Children:	Under the letter *f.* (Child puts the word on the wall.)
Teacher:	Put it under the picture of the fish — *f.*
Teacher:	Generated several sentences containing the word *for.*

Note that in this first grade example the teacher is attending to the formation of the letters as she is teaching the new word. Formation of letters is an important part of letter learning. In order to be fluent writers, children need to be able to form the letters of the words they are writing quickly without attending to how they are made. Your informal observations of your students when they are writing will tell you how much formation practice they will need.

Grade 2: Dialogue with the Class on Learning the Word *could* (*old* was already on the word wall)

Teacher:	This is a word I've noticed many of you having trouble with in your writing. The word is *could.* (Writes the word *could* on an overhead or on the board.) Have any of you had trouble reading this word in books? Can you think of a book where you saw it?
Teacher:	Why do you think this word is trickier to learn than some other words we've learned?
Children:	There's an *l* in it that we can't hear.
Teacher:	In some words, there are letters you can't hear. This is one of them. What else do you notice?
Children:	It has two vowels in the middle.
Teacher:	That's right. You can see the *o* and the *u* together, but do they make separate sounds?
Children:	No.
Teacher:	Right. And this is a word that has letters in it that you don't hear, so this is a word that has a part that is easy to confuse. Can you find a word on the word wall that might look similar and cause you confusion?
Children:	I think maybe *old.* It kind of looks like the last part of *could.*
Teacher:	Good noticing, and that's what I see some of you doing in your writing. You're writing *cold* when you mean to write *could. Cold* starts like *could* and ends like *could*, but what's different? (The teacher masks *co* and *ld.*)
Children:	*Could* has a *u* in it.

Teacher:	Right. And that's why the sound of the middle part of the word changes. Let's use this word in a sentence. "We could play a game if we finish our work." (The teacher says the sentence and has the children repeat it.)
Teacher:	Let's spell the word. *C-o-u-l-d.* Let's spell it again. *C-o-u-l-d.* Now write it on your paper.
Teacher:	(The teacher writes *could* on a card and selects a child to place it on the word wall.) I expect you to use this word on the word wall in your reading and writing.
Teacher:	Can you think of other words this word would help you to read and write?
Children:	*Should, would.* What about *couldn't?*
Teacher:	That's right. Now you see how you can use the word wall to help you with the tricky parts in your reading and writing.

Notice the many different ways the teachers attended to the word and had the children practice. The teacher: used the word in context; directed their attention to the visual form of the word; provided opportunity for kinesthetic practice of the word (snap, clap, and write); and helped them to see the connection between the new word and a word they already know.

Putting Generative Words on the Wall

Teaching a Principle of How Words Work

Helping children learn to use words on the wall to make analogies to new words is critical. Research has found "…that children make analogies between letter sequences representing rimes (*ump* in *jump*) significantly better than they make analogy between letter sequences representing phonemes that are parts of rimes (*u-m-p* in *jump*)" (Moustafa 1997, p. 46). The power of using analogy is not in learning every member of a word family but in teaching children *how to* use a generative principle.

Reviewing records of oral reading and writing samples will help you decide which principle (see Chapter 3) needs to be explicitly taught in a whole group mini-lesson.

Dialogue: How One Principle Might be Taught

Teacher:	Today we're going to talk about one way you can use words on the wall to help you get to new words you need to know.

Teacher:	You can use a word that you know, like *can*, to read or write another word that ends with the same letters. (The teacher places magnetic letters for the word *can* on the overhead projector and underneath them places the letters for the word *man*.)
Teacher:	This word is *man*. What part of these words is the same?
Children:	The last part.
Teacher:	That's right. (The teacher moves the letter *c* away from *an* and slides it back, saying the word slowly without a break. Then the teacher does the same for *man*.) They look the same and they sound the same at the end.
Teacher:	What part looks different?
Children:	The first letter.
Teacher:	(Places the letters for the word *ran* on an overhead.) If the first word is *can* and the second word is *man*, can you tell me what the last word is?
Children:	*Ran.*
Teacher:	Right. Do you see how you can look for a part you know in a word and change the first letter to get a new word?
Teacher:	(Removes all but one *an* chunk and places the letters *c*, *m*, and *r* to the left of the *an* chunk. She invites two children to come up and make the known word and then change the first letter to make one of the new words. Then she invites the other child to change the first letter back to make the known word and then make the other new word.)

known → new → known → new
can → man → can → ran

At this point the teacher might choose another known word and use the same procedure. It is unnecessary to teach every possibility (every member of the word family). What is important is that the children understand how to use a known word or part of that word to figure out a new word.

Ongoing Assessment

Weekly word wall checks will help you determine which children have learned the words from the whole group setting and which children need more direct instruction in a small group. Children who need more instruction often need to learn how to learn a word. Some children find it easy to learn a word, while others experience some difficulty. It is not about how many words children have learned, but whether their brains develop the ability to cognitively hold on to visual aspects of words so that they are retrieved with little conscious attention at any time in reading and writing. The goal should be automaticity and fluency.

Writing samples will give you some indication of how the children are taking on new words. Records of oral reading will also tell if new words are coming into the children's reading vocabulary. Weekly word wall checks provide the quickest and easiest method of finding out if the new words are being learned.

A weekly word wall check might look like this:
- Turn the children away from the wall.
- Choose five to ten words (early on it would be five) that you believe most children have managed to learn.
- Dictate these words and have the children write them quickly.
- Collect the lists for assessment.

Look for children who can write 80 to 90 percent of the words. They do not need further small group instruction but will benefit from reinforcement in a word study center. Be attentive to children who still use sound analysis as their predominant means of spelling. These children need to work toward more fluent and automatic production of the words.

Children who are having difficulty with learning high frequency words will have trouble learning how to use analogy effectively. Some of them have not yet learned how to learn words. You will want to plan small group activities to help them with this skill before you support them in using analogy (see Chapter 5).

Retiring Words From the Word Wall

If all of your students know certain words based on word wall checks, the words can be retired (removed) from the wall. Words need to be continually added to and deleted from the word wall so that there are not too many words on the wall at any given time. The wall should never become visually overwhelming. Some teachers find it helpful to keep retired words stored somewhere near the word wall for additional practice. We have seen teachers store retired words in a separate box or in a library pocket under the word wall. Teachers need to make children aware of the progress they are making in learning the words by engaging them in a dialogue that might sound like this:

Boys and girls, I have noticed that all of you know how to write and read several of the words on our wall. We're going to take them off the wall to make room for new words that will be useful for you to know. Today we are taking down three words. Which ones do you think we should take down?

The teacher and students engage in a conversation about which words should come down, but the teacher has final say about which words are removed. It is important to discuss with the children where removed words will be stored and how they can be used.

"No Excuse Words" Chart

At times there will be words that have been removed because children have shown they know them in a series of word wall checks, but the teacher notices that they are still misspelled in the children's writing. The teacher can construct a chart of a few of these words that have previously been removed from the word wall. This device is known as a "No Excuse Words" Chart. Teachers have found it helpful to put transparencies of children's writing on the overhead to show how these known words are still being misspelled. By focusing on a couple of these words at a time, the children's attention is directed to checking their own writing.

5 Practicing the Words on the Wall

Whole Group Activities

Plan a daily activity for the whole class to practice newly presented word wall words. The importance of these daily activities is that the children learn to look to the wall as a reference tool as well as learning the words. Here are a few favorites of the teachers we work with.

Words of the Week

- Once the new words for the week have been placed on the word wall, draw attention to them with highlighter tape. This way the words you are working on for the week will be easier for the children to find.
- For younger students, have an additional special place in the room where the new words are displayed weekly. (A good place might be near the alphabet/word study center.) Ask the children to read and spell the words to themselves whenever they have a chance.
- Have the children practice finding the words on the wall. This helps them learn to use the header cards to locate specific words.
- After the new words of the week are on the board, have the children clap and chant the words as they spell them. An alternative would be to snap their fingers.
  (See the dialogue on Page 19.)

I Spy

- Many teachers use this popular game. It helps children locate the words on the wall and learn them.
- Begin by saying the phrase, "I spy with my little eye, a word wall word that…"
  Use one of the phrases below to complete your sentence.
  - begins like _____
  - ends like _____
  - rhymes with _____
- Once a child has guessed the word, the teacher points to the word on the wall and has all the children spell it in unison.

Crosschecking with the Word Wall

- The teacher writes the first letter of a word from the word wall. Then he or she says a sentence and leaves out the word.
  - Write the letter *b* on the board.
  - Say, "The word begins with *b* and fits in this sentence. I like to bounce my _____ on the driveway."

Guess the Word

- The teacher chooses five words and tells the children they will have to guess the words.
- Each child gets a paper and pencil.
- The teacher writes the first letter of one of the words.
- The children write their guesses on their papers.
- The teacher writes another letter. The children check to see if they got the second letter correct; if not, they make another guess.
- The teacher writes the next letter. The children check and make another guess if they need to.
- Continue until the word is on the board. Ask how many children guessed the word on the first try, the second try, etc.
- Have all children spell and say the word.
- Repeat the game with the next word.

Wordo

This version of bingo is a favorite with children. Each child will need a piece of paper on which squares are drawn. Use 4 squares for kindergarten, 9 for first grade, and 25 for second grade (see Appendix B, pages 52-54). Wordo works best in a small group setting with kindergarten children.

me	the
can	to

- Call on a child to pick four words from the word wall, one at a time. The child spells the words. Everyone writes those four words in any square they choose. All the students will have the same words on their paper, but in different squares.
- While the students are writing the words on their papers, the teacher writes them on index cards.
- The teacher shuffles the index cards and the game begins.
- The teacher draws and calls out the word on that card.
- The children chant the spelling of the word and cover it with a small object.
- The child who covers a complete row first wins.
- The children clear their sheets and another round of Wordo begins. (The winner of one game can be the caller for the next round.)

   Adapted from *Phonics They Use*, Cunningham (1995).

Word Wall Stories

Encourage the children to write stories using word wall words. At sharing time, as a child reads his or her story, encourage the rest of the children to listen carefully and raise their hands when they hear a word wall word.

The Chain Game

- The children in Jane Cutler's class in Dennis-Yarmouth, Massachussets designed this game. It can be adapted to whole group, small group, or learning center practice.
- The children are given a piece of paper and a pencil.
- The teacher or child chooses a word wall word and everyone writes it on the paper.
- The last letter of the word is circled.
- The teacher then has the children find a word that begins with the circled letter at the end of the last word.
- The last letter in this word is circled and the next word begins with that letter.
- The teacher can continue with as many words as time allows.
- As a variation, you could have a child search and choose the next word.

Check that Rime

An overhead projector and transparency are needed for this activity (see Appendix B, Page 55).

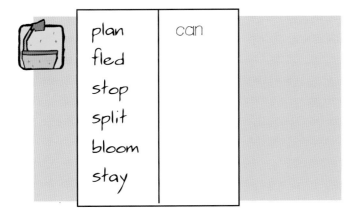

The teacher writes the word on the transparency in the left column and then reads the word or asks a child to read the word. The children then search the word wall for the word with the same rime. Once the word is found, a child is chosen to write the word in the right column. This is a good way to use words with blends and clusters that the children may not yet have encountered in their reading.

Small Group Teacher-Directed Instruction

For those children who need more intensive guided instruction, small group lessons should be planned regularly. You need to consider whether or not your struggling students have learned how to learn a word or whether they just need more concentrated practice of the words.

Many students who seem to have difficulty remembering words have not yet learned how to look at a word carefully enough to see its significant features and remember them. Records of oral reading will quickly help you identify who might still need to learn how to learn a word. Look for substitutions (miscues) on high frequency words you know have been previously taught and practiced. Below is a sample of this type of record.

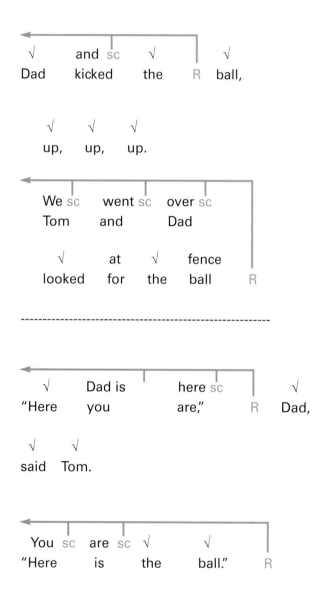

Although the child's language has supported his predictions, in this record of oral reading we can see some remaining confusions with *and*, *for*, *is*, and *are*. The goal for high frequency words is that the child knows them so well that they require little attention. This now frees up the child's mind to focus on more complex words such as *fence* and *ball*.

A small group lesson to help students learn how to learn a word would include some or all of these components:

Magnetic letters

    a. The teacher puts letters for the word *and* on the magnetic board and says, "This is the way *and* looks."

    b. The teacher leaves the word visible and gives the children additional letters and asks them to make the word *and*.

    c. The teacher takes the model away and asks the children to mix up their letters and construct the word *and* again. This can be done as many times as needed.

    d. Subsequently, the teacher could give the children the letters and say, "Use these letters to make a word you know and tell me what it is."

Writing

    a. The teacher writes the word first.

    b. Then the children write the word in the air, on the rug, or on an individual chalkboard or whiteboard.

Visualization

    a. The teacher writes the word.

    b. The teacher says the word while running a finger under it (left to right).

    c. The teacher asks the children to say the word and look at how it starts, what's in the middle, and how it ends.

    d. The teacher directs the children to close their eyes and make a picture of the word in their mind. The teacher then asks the children if they can "see the word in their mind."

    e. The teacher covers the model and asks the children to open their eyes and write the word on their chalkboards.

    f. This procedure may have to be repeated several times until the children learn how to look at the features of words closely enough to remember them easily.

Fluent Writing

    a. Once children can write words correctly, they can be encouraged to build speed and bring words to automaticity.

Children need to have automatic recognition of a word. For some this is easy and they can learn a word with very little practice. Many children need many different types of practice where the teacher gradually lessens support in order to encourage the children to learn words.

The continuum below describes instruction for learning words in small groups. Teacher support gradually lessens along this continuum. How much support does a particular group of children need in order to learn words? You may have to start at the top of the continuum and work down through each of the activities over several days. You may be able to skip some of the activities if a group seems to be able to construct words more independently.

Instructional Continuum for Learning Words in Small Groups

The teacher constructs the word with magnetic letters and tells the word.

The teacher supplies the letters for the word and tells the word to be constructed. The children construct the word and check it by running a finger under the word while saying it.

The teacher supplies the letters for the new word and tells the children to "make a word you know." The children construct the word and check it by running a finger under the word while saying it.

The teacher supplies a pool of letters for several words the children have been working on and names the word to be constructed. The children construct a word, and then read and check it. Then they write the word several times on a whiteboard

The teacher supplies the pool of letters and tells the children to "make a word you know." The children construct a word, and then read and check it. Then they write the word several times on a whiteboard. (Note: Different children may be constructing different words.)

The teacher dictates the word. The children write the word, and then read and check it.

The teacher can dictate any word and the children write it quickly and easily.

One way to teach a small group using this continuum is to provide every child with a small magnetic whiteboard and magnetic letters for the words being learned. Notice that the continuum begins with a teacher demonstration and gradually releases responsibility for the task to the child. If the word is new, the teacher provides a clear demonstration. If this is a word the children have worked on before, you may choose to work further down on the continuum.

Many of the activities we suggest for whole group and learning center activities can be adapted to small groups. There are many other activities that can be used for effective small group practice. One such resource is *Making Your Word Wall More Interactive*, by Trisha Callella (2001). Another is *Word Solvers: Making Sense of Letters and Sounds*, by Michèle DuFresne (2002). The activities in these resource guides and others will give your students appropriate practice in word learning.

Literacy Center Activities

Literacy centers provide opportunities for children to independently practice what has already been taught in whole and small group settings. This is meaningful practice that can be completed without teacher assistance and allows children to become proficient in all areas of learning going on in the classroom. More information about literacy centers can be found in *Guided Reading & Literacy Centers* (2003) and *Literacy Centers for the Primary Classroom* (1999), both published by Dominie Press.

The purpose of word work in centers is to give children the additional practice they need to use the words and principles you have taught in a whole and small group setting. Many of the activities used in whole and small group practice can be adapted for use in literacy centers.

To support this learning, we suggest some of the following activities. You may choose many more activities for word practice, but remember the focus of these activities should be on the words and principles you are teaching.

Reading and Writing Activities
- Read the word wall *A-Z* with a friend. Then read it backwards.
- Make five word wall words with magnetic letters. Write them in your word study notebook.

Word Wall – ABC Order
- Write the words that are on the word wall on little cards and place them in an envelope in your alphabet/word study center.
- The children can take the cards out, put them in *A-B-C* order, and then read them.

- Variations:

    Alphabetize the words to the second letter, third letter, etc.

    - Ask the children to choose a letter and then write all the words for that letter in their word study notebooks.
    - Tell the children to find five words that are hard to remember. Have them practice saying the words and writing them in their word study notebooks.

My Name on the Wall (See Appendix B, Page 56.)

- Prepare sheets that can be left in the center. The children write their names, letter by letter, in the blanks on the left side of the page. They then search for and write words next to each letter that start like the letters in their names. They can then highlight the first letter in each word and they will have their name spelled (downward) several times.

C	**c**an	**c**ut	**c**ould
A	**a**nd	**a**t	**a**sk
T	**t**o	**t**he	**t**hat
E	**e**ach	**e**very	**e**nter

Spell My Word

- Two can play this game. Prepare some small letter cards (one for each letter) and put them in a small plastic bag.
- Child # 1 draws a letter card from the bag and shows it to Child # 2.
- Child #2 chooses a word from the word wall that begins with that letter. Child #2 asks Child # 1 to spell the word.
- If Child # 1 spells the word correctly, he or she gets to keep the card.
- The roles are reversed, and Child #2 has the opportunity to spell a word.
- The child with the most letter cards at the end wins the game.

Making Connections With Word Wall Words

Use some of the following sheets to help children practice writing word wall words and then make connections to other word wall words. (See Appendix B, pages 57 and 58, for copies of these sheets.)

In this activity, the children choose some word wall words and write them down the middle of the chart. The first and last columns are then filled in. Activities like this also support the children in learning how to search the word wall for words they need.

Begins Like...	Word Wall Word	Ends Like...

In this activity, the children would write the week's highlighted words on the sheet first. The last column is a challenge that asks the children to come up with a word that rhymes and probably is not on the word wall.

Write Your Word	Begins Like...	Ends Like...	Rhymes with...
1.			
2.			
3.			
4.			
5.			
6.			
7.			

The following activities help older children look for similar vowels and vowel patterns in word wall words (see Appendix B, pages 59 and 60).

Choose a short vowel. I choose_____ .
Find all the words on the word wall that have this short vowel sound.

_____ _____ _____

_____ _____ _____

_____ _____ _____

Write a sentence using one of the words you wrote.

_____

_____

Choose a long vowel. I choose_____ .
Find all the words on the word wall that have this long vowel sound.

_____ _____ _____

_____ _____ _____

_____ _____ _____

Write a sentence using one of the words you wrote.

_____

_____

Making Analogies With Word Wall Words

Roll It – Name It – Write It

Prepare some rime dice by writing on the sides of a small block some of the rimes you have taught in connection with the word wall (see Appendix B, Page 61) .

- Two children can play this game; they take turns rolling the dice and recording the answers.
- The dice is rolled. The rime is recorded in the first column.
- The children search the word wall for a word with that rime and write it in the second column.
- Then they have to think of another word that has the same rime and write it in the third column.

Rime	Word Wall Word	Another Word

Changing Word Wall Words

Children can be challenged to use analogy and change the beginning and ending of word wall words using a sheet like the one below (see Appendix B, Page 62). This activity can be worked on collaboratively or individually.

I can turn word wall words into other words by changing the beginning letters.		
This Word Wall Word	Can Change Into	This New Word
	→	
	→	

The same type of activity sheet can be used for changing the ends of words (see Appendix B, Page 63).

" Have A Go" Card

This activity is adapted from *Ideas for Spelling* (Bolton and Snowball, 1993).

Children can use the "Have a Go" cards for trying words they want to use in their writing but are not sure they know how to spell correctly (see Appendix B, Page 64). Teachers can have these cards available as a tool for children to use in a writing center. One example might look like this.

1st Try	2nd Try	Correct Spelling	Copied Spelling

Child attempts spelling

Child attempts spelling with revisions

Child checks word with word wall first and then with teacher if the word is not on the wall

Child practices writing correct word using the "look, cover, write, check" procedure

Look, Cover, Write, Check
- **Look** at the word and say it.
- **Cover** the word.
- **Write** the word as a whole unit (not letter by letter).
- **Check** spelling. If incorrect, repeat procedure.

"Have a Go" Cards encourage children to recommend words that might be added to the word wall. Consider having a recommendation box somewhere in your classroom. The children can write the word on a card and explain why they are recommending it.

Teachers must plan activities that invite students to develop deeper understandings of the relationships between letters and sounds and that explicitly show them how to use word parts as springboards for reading and spelling other words. These activities, as well as many others you may try, help children not only build a reading and writing vocabulary, but also gain an understanding of how words work.

6 Taking the Words off the Wall

Everything that we've discussed about word walls so far leads to one goal—that at some point students become empowered to independently take words apart in reading and construct words in writing.

The foundation that was constructed by the word wall works in:
- Whole class demonstrations and activities.
- Direct, explicit instruction in small groups.
- Independent practice in word study centers.

This provides the necessary tools to allow students to become successful processors of print. Given that this earlier teaching is with isolated words taken out of context, a shift now needs to occur so that children can develop the ability to automatically make analogies while reading and writing text.

Word walls provide an engaging, temporary scaffold as children learn:
- How to learn a word.
- Use an analogy.
- Make connections.

Now the teacher needs to literally help the children take the learning that has surrounded word wall work "off the wall."

Reading and writing assessments help the teacher see where individual children are on their journey to independent processing of print. Ongoing analysis of records of oral reading helps teachers to identify when children have started to do this visual analysis "on the run."

Taking the words off the wall is not a physical activity any longer, but more a cognitive ability children have gained that allows them to internalize the processes of making connections and using analogy. With skillful prompting, the teacher now serves as a coach and supports all independent moves initiated by the children.

Students may be able to use word wall words to make analogies out of context, but they may not yet see those parts in extended text. The ability to notice larger chunks of visual information in text is a critical milestone on the way to successful visual processing. At first the teacher must demonstrate and show the child the part to be noticed and then prompt for use of analogy.

The teacher might do this by writing the word part on a whiteboard or by covering all but the part to be highlighted with a finger. The goal of these demonstrations is to enable the child to begin looking for known parts in words so an analogy can be made.

In the following example of an oral reading record, the child is not attempting more than sounding the initial letter. Helping to identify a known word part in text and then to make an analogy using a word wall word is the first step in helping a child use larger chunks of visual information when reading text.

To continue to foster independent word analysis, the teacher might encourage the child to look for a known part by saying:

"What do you notice about this word? Does it remind you of another word you know?"

"What part of the word might help you?"

  √   √ √ √ √
Jonathan cut out the tail.

 √ √ √   √   √
Then he made some fins.

 √ √   √ s- s- sp-sp A
and some round spots.

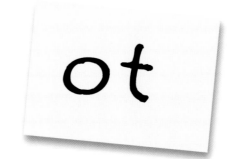

ot

Teacher: Remember how you have made new words using a word you know from the word wall. You know something about this word. This word (*spots*) is like *got* on our word wall.
(The teacher writes the word part *ot* on the whiteboard and shows it to the child.)

Teacher: Now start back here (points to the beginning of the sentence) and think about how this part will help you figure out that tricky word.

Child: (The child rereads the sentence: "Then he made some fins and some round sp-ots/spots.") The teacher may choose to reread the sentence with the child and begin to articulate the word, fading as the child says the word.

Teacher: Good. You noticed the letter *s* on the end of *spots* and you used a word you know to help you figure out this word you weren't sure of.

Once children understand the idea of looking for parts that might be helpful, the next shift toward independence occurs when the teacher demonstrates using a finger to highlight the part to be noticed. Sometimes two fingers have to be used if there is an inflectional ending. The child needs to be able to see the helpful part quickly.

When the teacher is able to isolate the word part without any verbal prompts and the child quickly identifies the word, the child can be prompted to do this on his or her own.

Teacher:	You know this part. (The teacher covers *st* with one finger and *ed* with another.)
Child:	Art.
Teacher:	(The teacher removes a finger from *st*.)
Child:	St-art.
Teacher:	(The teacher removes a finger from *ed*.)
Child:	Started.

This is done very quickly, and the teacher encourages the child to reread when necessary to maintain meaning.

Children who can locate helpful parts on their own routinely, need to be prompted to initiate a flexible way of processing by just using their eyes. At first the teacher has to determine the most productive prompt that leads the child to solve the word quickly.

Scenario One

The child is aware there's an error.

√   √   √   √
"My   rabbit   has   gone!

√   √   √
It   has   gone!"

√   √   √
said   the   lion.

√   √   h-√   √   starve   √
And   he   had   to   stay   hungry.

If a child does not stop at the point of error, the teacher lets the child get to the end of the page (or paragraph).

Teacher:	You did a nice job. Can you show me the word that tricked you on this page?
Child:	(The child points to the word *stay*.)
Teacher:	Check how that word ends. You know something about it.
Child:	(The child reads *st-ay* and rereads the sentence.)

Scenario Two

The child doesn't realize he's made an error. (Often the substitution is meaningful.)

√   √   √ √   √
Danny   looked   at   the   clock.

√ √   √
It was 5:30.

√   √   √   √
"I'm   hungry,"   said   Danny.

√   √   √
"How   much   longer

√ √   √   √   watch
do I have to wait?"

Teacher: There was something that tricked you on this page. Read it again and check how the words end.

Child: (The child rereads the page and corrects the error: "How much longer to I have to w-ait?")

Scenario Three

Later, when the child has become more independent, several prompts might be used to encourage flexibility in solving the word. In this instance, the child is required to select what will help solve the difficulty in the most efficient manner.

√   √   was want went SC √   √
Mrs. Pig wanted   her friends

√   √   √   √   √
to come to picnic lunch.

√   √   √   √   √
She called and asked them.

√   √   soup spices
She made sandwiches.

Teacher: Does that word look like what you read?
Does it make sense in this text?
What do you know about this word?
Can you look at the word and start to say it?

The teacher needs to be flexible with questions to initiate problem solving, and if one doesn't work, he or she should be ready to try another one that might be more meaningful for the child. The key is to find just the right support for fast, efficient problem solving by the child.

Independent Problem Solving

Students who can solve words independently and have become automatic processors of print could have records of oral reading that look like this. (Note how the child attempts to maintain meaning while problem solving.)

√   √   √   √   want R SC   √
One day Mr. Cricket went   looking

(The child knew *want* didn't sound right and checked through the word.)

√   √   √   √   √   √
for   a   new   place   to   live.

√   found went SC   √   √
He   wanted   a   place

(The child used story meaning to predict *found* and then checked to see how the word looked to self-correct.)

√   √   √   √   √
that   was   safe   and   warm.

√   √   √   √   √
He   crawled   under   the   door

√ R   √   √   √
of   a   big   R   house.

(The child reread to confirm, making sure the text still made sense.)

√   help hop SC   √   √   c-c-corn-√
He   hopped   into   a   corner

(The child initially used phonics when saying *help* but used story meaning to self-correct.)

√   √   √
in   the   kitchen,

√   √   √   √   √
but   Dad   swept   him   out.

√   √   √   √   √   √
He   hopped   into   the   toy   box

√   √   √
in   the   playroom,

(The child read accurately and fluently.)

√   √   √   √   √   √
but the children tipped him out.

√   √   √   √   √   box bas-ket SC
He hopped into the cat's basket,

(The child made a meaningful first attempt and then self-corrected.)

√   √   √   √   √   √
but the cat nearly ate him.

√   √   √   √   √
He hopped into the bathtub,

√   √   √ wash-√ √ √
but Mom nearly washed him away.

(The child quickly looked to the end of the word.)

√   √   √   √
Mr. Cricket was sad.

√   √ √ √ √ √
Where can I find a home

that's sc the sc √ √ √
that   is   R safe and warm?

(The child self-corrected when the text didn't sound right.)

√   √   √ was SC √ sm-√ √
Just then he saw   a small hole

(The child searched the word left to right and self-corrected.)

√ √   √
in the fireplace.

It sc l-ast √ √ √
At   last R he had found

(The child checked the first word more carefully, decoded the second word using onset and rime, and reread to confirm the meaning.)

√   √ √   √   √
what he was looking for

√ f-ine √ √
— a fine new home.

Word wall work also supports the child's ability to write words quickly and construct new ones. Fluent processing needs to occur not only in reading, but also in writing. The word wall supports this learning by giving children the opportunity to learn to write many high frequency words quickly and fluently.

> *"Knowing many words makes it easier to write stories because much of the text is written quickly, which frees the attention to go to new words that the child does have to work on" (Clay, 2001, p. 24).*

> *"Knowing many different words enlarges one's chances of getting to new words" (Clay, 2001, p. 24).*

Children need to have a wide range of known words in order to be able to use the generating principle effectively. Once many different words are known, using these words from the word wall also supports children in their attempts to construct more difficult words in their writing.

The following examples show when children did not use one of the principles in their writing and dialogue of what the teaching around the difficulty would look like.

Not using correct rime (see Page 16)

The child writes: I am going to lak (lock) the door.

Teacher:	I like the way you tried to write that sentence by yourself. Was there a tricky word?
Child:	(Child points to *lak.*)
Teacher:	Find a word on the word wall that ends with the same sound as *lock.*
Child:	*Sock* ends like *lock.* (Writes *lock* correctly.)
Teacher:	Does that word look right to you now?

Not using correct inflectional ending (see Page 16)

The child writes: My sister helpt (helped) me with my reading.

Teacher:	Was there a tricky word in that sentence for you to write?
Child:	(Child points to *helpt.*)
Teacher:	Show me with your finger the part that doesn't look right to you.
Child:	(The child isolates the letter *t.*)
Teacher:	That's right. You know the chunk *-ed.*

(Teacher writes -*ed* on the whiteboard.)

Sometimes it sounds like a *t*, but it's spelled -*ed*.

More attention needs to be given to the middle of the word (see Page 17)

The child writes: The boy scribbled (scrambled) out from under the *bushes.*

Teacher: I noticed you hesitated on this word. (Indicates *scribbled.*) Show me the part that doesn't look right to you.

Child: (The child isolates the middle of the word with two fingers.)

Teacher: Say the word slowly and listen for the sounds in the middle of that word.

Child: (The child says the word slowly) "*Am* is in the middle," (writes *scrambled* correctly).

Teacher: Remember, you can figure out many words by saying them slowly and listening for parts you know.

Note: Children have to be able to say a word slowly in syllables, think about a part they hear, and relate it to something they already know.

The child's message is: I am looking up information on the Internet.

The child asks for help on the word *information.*

Teacher: What can you do to help yourself now?

Child: (The child shrugs.)

Teacher: You could clap the syllables and listen for parts that are like ones you already know. Try that.

Child: (The child claps and writes each syllable as he says it.)

Teacher: I like the way you figured that word out by yourself.

Child: (The child applies the same principle to *Internet* and writes it successfully.)

Children also are helped in their writing when they understand that there are different categories of words in English (Clay, 1993, p. 35).

1. Sometimes you have to remember what a word looks like.
2. You can write a new word through analogy, using a common spelling pattern.
3. You can sound a word out slowly and write the sounds you hear.

The word wall supports work with the first two categories. Children will learn high frequency words and how to use analogy during daily word wall work. However, teachers need to be aware that additional instruction is needed with the third category (You can sound a word out slowly and write the sounds you hear). This is especially important when we ask children to analyze longer words syllable by syllable, as in the last example. Children must first show proficiency in hearing and recording sounds in sequential order for simple words before they can analyze multi-syllable words. Once this learning is in place and the children understand the concept of analogy, they can easily begin to write multi-syllable words.

It is often helpful to look at children's writing samples while keeping these three categories in mind. Looking at writing samples, especially of older readers, will help you decide what kind of teaching about these categories still needs to occur. It is often very difficult to look at a piece of writing and know where to begin. Here we share a sample of writing where support is needed in all three categories.

After analyzing the following piece, it is evident that Amanda, a third grader, could use support in thinking about all three of the categories. The teacher will have to decide which is the most profitable for Amanda now as a developing writer.

The Gift of Sacred Dog By Paul Gobb
Retold By Amanda

Long a go thar was a groop of
natev amarkins cald the people and
one day all the bufflow hairds
were kild for th horns an met
and skin and bons sq for a very
long time the people were storving
almost to death, until one day
a boy from the crude of tpes
Said I'am going to the mounting
and I'am going to fide the great
god, I will be back in the moring
So the boy set off for his Jurny
when he got to the top of the
moutin he seid please great god
help my people they are starving
my brothers and sisters ore sick
and my mom and dad gave all the
food to my brother and sister Sunde
thurnder binds sweept out of the clou
and their eys were red and thar wi
woshed like thurnder then the god
Spook I now your People are starving
so take thes sackret doga they w
help you find plenty of food for yo

Category #1
Here are some samples of words that Amanda may have been able to spell correctly if she had said them slowly to herself.

moutin	fide	moring	sundely	thurnder
mountain	find	morning	suddenly	thunder

Category #2
These are words that Amanda should be able to write quickly and automatically.

thar	crucle	seid	now	thees
there	circle	said	know	these

Category #3
The last category includes words Amanda could have gotten successfully through analogy.

groop	natev	cald	hairds	bons	tpes	spook
group	native	called	herds	bones	teepees	spoke

Just as reading requires use of the word wall to take words apart on the run while reading, it also enables children to quickly construct words they want or need to write. By demonstrating how the word wall supports both reading texts and writing messages, an informed teacher can successfully turn over these tasks to the students and enable greater independence over time.

Older Readers and Special Needs Children – Q&A

What do I do with students in second grade and beyond who were not taught how to read and write using a word wall?

We'd start with assessment. Find out what they know. Recommendations for assessment would be having them read and write a list of words frequently encountered in print. There are many lists available. You will have to decide which ones and how many to use. The *Dominie Reading & Writing Assessment Portfolio* (DeFord, 2001) includes a spelling assessment that can be used for this purpose. Take stock of which words the children have managed to learn. This will help you determine whether they have learned how to learn a word.

Give a dictation sentence such as the ones found in the *Dominie Reading & Writing Assessment Portfolio*. This will help you determine whether children can hear sounds and record the appropriate letters in sequence, and whether they are taking on conventional spelling patterns appropriate for their grade level.

Here are some examples of these sentences:

Grade two: *Once my pet snake followed a baby skunk under the garage. Slinky tried to catch the skunk, but he was very smelly.*

Grade three: *The newspaper showed the two trains jammed up close at the crossing. It seems the crash started as an ice car came loose.*

Grade four: *The beaches were deserted before midnight and the moon glowed brightly. Floating undisturbed in the breeze, the empty skiff caught the swells that brought it gently to the dark shore.*

Grade five: *A hurricane was brewing off the coast of Fiji. Satellites tracked the tropical storm. In the ocean, Coast Guard cruisers hailed two fishing trawlers and issued orders to head in to shore.*

Children in the second grade and above often do not understand how to use analogy when decoding words. It's important, then, to find out which principles they can use. Which ones do they know, and which ones have to be taught?

Another option is to take a record of oral text reading to see how children take words apart in text. Are they using syllables and larger chunks of visual information as they take words apart "on the run?"

Look across all of these assessments and use this information to determine what each child has managed to learn so far. Based on what you discover, plan for teacher-directed instruction in small groups and individual practice. Personal word walls in a manila folder are especially helpful with older readers.

Does this kind of instruction work with children who have special needs, or do they require a different approach?

We think all children can learn about words and how they work using a word wall. Special needs children may need a longer time to transition through learning how to learn a word and then work through each principle. It is important to keep the core of words they are working on relatively small. New words should be added judiciously, and the Instructional Continuum for Learning Words should be kept in mind.

If word cards are used, have each child work with only five to six words at a time. Keep in mind what is known, what is partially known, and what is new. Consider adjusting the way you remove a known word to make room for a new word.

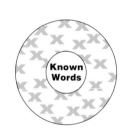

Looking at this graphic of a circle within a circle, you can see that it would be difficult for children who are challenged in learning to be able to gain control of new words when they have so many partially known words to deal with. In this graphic, all the *X*s represent partially known words. If there are too many partially known words floating around in a child's head, it becomes a very difficult task for that child to recall and use them in reading and writing.

Only when a solid core of words has been mastered can children begin to see and use analogies. We have found that it is better to give these learners the time they need and follow their lead before progressing to the next step of learning about analogies.

It is important that children come across known words in the text they are reading and that they see these words written in modeled and interactive writing.

Is there a place for word walls in the upper grades? If so, what would they look like?

Yes. As we pointed out earlier, exemplars of higher-level rimes with silent letters can be used, as well as any of the following types of words.

- Homonyms, homophones – *grate, great*
- Words that have subtle differences – *angel, angle*
- Multi-syllabic words that are frequently misspelled – *because*
- Uncommon onsets - *know, gnat*
- Common foreign words – *blasé, faux pas, fait accompli*
- Commonly confused spelling patterns – *changeable, lovable*

Attention needs to be drawn to where multi-syllabic words are broken so that children will be able to quickly use analogy and take words apart during on-the-run reading.

A third or fourth grade word wall would look substantially different from a first grade word wall. Fourth graders will have learned how to learn a word. Now we're showing them how to see subtle differences in the spelling of words like *though, through, thorough, and thought* while increasing their awareness of:

- unusual juxtaposition of letters within words (*weird, phlegm, bundt*)
- problematic spellings (*a lot, especially, February, answer*)
- categories for constructing plurals (*calf/calves, ox/oxen*)
- homographs (*bass, object, contest*)

An effective procedure that a teacher at this level might try is to sort out common confusions around triple homophones like *their, there,* and *they're*.

1. Have the class investigate how each of these words is used in a phrase or sentence. Divide the class into small groups (investigation teams) and send each team on a search to find examples of each homophone used in a sentence in print around the classroom. (*They put their book on the table*.) Have each investigation team record their examples on chart paper.
2. Display each team's chart and highlight the most interesting examples.
3. Ask each group individually to formulate a clear definition for each of the triple homophones, using the chart's they constructed.
4. Now add each homophone to the word wall, listing them together.

Often students are aware of the correct spellings and appropriate use of these kinds of words, but this understanding is not demonstrated in their writing. We believe that this transfer will not occur until concepts like these are explored in depth in the context of whole and small group instruction (refer to the Instructional Continuum for Learning Words in Small Groups, Page 30).

Word walls at fourth grade and above can perform other functions for learners: As a thesaurus, they are a powerful vehicle for developing new vocabulary. They also allow students to be immersed in sorting out complex characters (such as in Shakespeare) or understanding specialized vocabulary in a text (Johnny Tremain).

Word walls also can be used to give children experiences with:
• classical reference – words from Latin and Greek mythology
• entomology – the study of word origins
• Greek and Latin roots and word parts

> *"The word wall is built on a spiral theory of mastery – repetition reinforces previously learned principles. Regular use throughout the school year allows you to recycle many words"* (Green, 1993, p. 11).

 I'm a reading specialist, and I travel from room to room in an elementary school. How can I use word walls effectively?

This can be accomplished by working closely with each classroom teacher. Realize that having more than one word wall to focus on at any one time is not helpful for children. Using supporting work already established in a classroom is always good practice. By being aware of what the classroom word wall is like in each of the rooms you go into, you can use the words introduced there in your lessons. Consider using portable word walls mounted on tri-fold presentation boards. Small group, teacher-directed instruction in the classroom can provide further support for children who need the reinforcement. We believe word wall instruction is most profitable when it takes place in the children's classroom. The same idea of portable word walls works well in year-round school settings.

Appendix A

Coding Conventions for Records of Text Reading

Note: The samples used in this book were shared by teachers who were trained to take Running Records using Marie Clay's *Observation Survey of Early Literacy Achievement* (2002) and *Running Records for Classroom Teachers* (2000). The coding conventions in this appendix are those used in the records of oral text reading throughout this book.

√ √ √ √	**accurate reading**
Child: <u>want</u> Text: went	**incorrect response**
Child: <u>h-e-l-p-</u> Text: help	**sounding out letter by letter**
Child: <u>went / want</u> Text: wanted	**multiple attempts, incorrect response**
Child: <u>looked / like / SC</u> Text: liked	**error corrected, self-correction (SC)**
Child: <u>√ R √ √ R √</u> ⟵ Text: of a big house	**repetition and text rereading (R)**
Child: <u>s-s-sp-sp- A</u> Text: spots	**child appeals for help**
Child: <u>g-r-a-y- A</u> Text: gray T	**child appeals for help, teacher tells the word**

Appendix B
Reproducible Forms

Wordo

<table>
<tr><td></td><td></td></tr>
<tr><td></td><td></td></tr>
</table>

(This page may be reproduced for classroom use.)

Wordo

(This page may be reproduced for classroom use.)

Wordo

Check That Rime

My Name on the Wall

_____   _____   _____   _____

_____   _____   _____   _____

_____   _____   _____   _____

_____   _____   _____   _____

_____   _____   _____   _____

_____   _____   _____   _____

_____   _____   _____   _____

_____   _____   _____   _____

_____   _____   _____   _____

_____   _____   _____   _____

Name _____

Starts Like...	Word Wall Word	Ends Like...

(This page may be reproduced for classroom use.)

Name _____

Write Your Word	Begins Like…	Ends Like…	Rhymes with…
1.			
2.			
3.			
4.			
5.			

(This page may be reproduced for classroom use.)

Name _____

Choose a Short Vowel

Choose a short vowel. I choose _____.
Find all the words on the word wall that have this short vowel sound.

_____   _____   _____

_____   _____   _____

_____   _____   _____

_____   _____   _____

_____   _____   _____

Write a sentence using one of the words you wrote.

_____

_____

_____

Name _____

Choose a Long Vowel

Choose a long vowel. I choose _____.
Find all the words on the word wall that have this long vowel sound.

_____   _____   _____

_____   _____   _____

_____   _____   _____

_____   _____   _____

_____   _____   _____

Write a sentence using one of the words you wrote.

_____

_____

_____

Name _____

Roll It – Name It – Write It

Rime	Word Wall Word	Another Word

(This page may be reproduced for classroom use.)

Name _____

Changing Word Wall Words

I can turn word wall words into other words by changing the beginning letter/s.

This Word Wall Word	Can Change Into	This New Word
_____	⟶	_____
_____	⟶	_____
_____	⟶	_____
_____	⟶	_____
_____	⟶	_____
_____	⟶	_____
_____	⟶	_____
_____	⟶	_____
_____	⟶	_____
_____	⟶	_____

Name _____

Changing Word Wall Words

I can turn word wall words into other words by changing the ending letter/s.

This Word Wall Word	Can Change Into	This New Word
_____	⟶	_____
_____	⟶	_____
_____	⟶	_____
_____	⟶	_____
_____	⟶	_____
_____	⟶	_____
_____	⟶	_____
_____	⟶	_____
_____	⟶	_____
_____	⟶	_____
_____	⟶	_____

(This page may be reproduced for classroom use.)

Name _____

"Have A Go" Card

1st Try	2nd Try	Correct Spelling	Copied Spelling

Look, Cover, Write, Check

- **Look** at the word and say it.
- **Cover** the word.
- **Write** the word as a whole unit (not letter by letter).
- **Check** spelling. If incorrect, repeat procedure.

(This page may be reproduced for classroom use.)

Glossary

ABC Chart:	Alphabetic chart of 26 squares, each containing an upper and lower case letter and a picture representing a word that begins with that letter
Analogies:	Connections that are made by linking a known word or word part to an unknown word encountered while reading and writing
Assessment:	Data gathered in order to understand the strengths and needs of a student; data can include observations, formal and informal testing, and samples of student work
Exemplars:	Generative words on a word wall that children can use to problem solve while reading and writing
Fluency:	The ability to read quickly and accurately with phrasing and expression
Fluent Writing:	The ability to write high frequency words quickly
Generative Words:	Words that can help a reader/writer make connections that aid in solving unknown words
Guided Instruction:	A teaching strategy in which the instructor takes on the role of coach to make a reading or writing experience more accessible to children
Header Cards:	Alphabet cards placed on the top of each list of words on the word wall
High Frequency Words:	Words used commonly in spoken or written language
High Utility Words:	Words that occur very often in spoken or written language
Highlighter Tape:	Transparent tape that is used to point out a word or word part; similar to a highlighter pen in purpose
Individual Word Wall:	Words that have been retired from the word wall but may not yet be known by some children; words placed alphabetically in a manila folder
Informal Observations:	Observations of children engaged in everyday literacy activities
Interactive Writing:	A teaching method in which students and teacher negotiate what they are going to write and then share the pen to construct the message
Kinesthetic Practice:	The motor component of learning (for example, clapping parts of words)

Literacy Centers:
Independent tasks or activities that support classroom learning and require no teacher assistance; centers are used in classrooms as a way of managing small group reading activities

Mini-lessons:
Short, intense whole group lessons (15-20 minutes) on a reading or writing strategy; the focus is defined by ongoing assessment

Names Chart:
A list of the first names of the children in a K-1 classroom grouped alphabetically

"No Excuse Words" Chart:
A list of known words that teacher and children agree will be consistently spelled correctly

Onset:
The letter/s before the vowel in a syllable or single syllable word (c /at ch/at)

Record of Oral Reading:
An account of a student's reading behaviors recorded during the oral reading of a text

Rhyme:
Usually identical or sometimes very similar recurring final sounds in words

Rime:
A vowel and any following consonants of a syllable

Shared Reading:
A teaching method in which the teacher and children read together from a text that is visible to all

Sound-to-Letter Correspondence:
The ability to hear sounds and record letters while constructing text

Word Charts:
Consist of vocabulary words particular to a content area topic (science, social studies, math)

Words We Know Chart:
Precursor to a word wall and used mainly in kindergarten; as the list of known words increases, the words are transferred to the word wall

Bibliography

Ballance, A. (2000). *Polar Regions*. Carlsbad, CA: Dominie Press, Inc.

Bear, D., Invernizzi, M., Templeton, S., and Johnston, F. (1996). *Words Their Way: Word Study for Phonics, Vocabulary, and Spelling Instruction*. Columbus, OH: Merrill.

Blakemore, C., and Ramirez, B. (1999). *Literacy Centers for the Primary Classroom*. Carlsbad, CA: Dominie Press, Inc.

Bolton, F., and Snowball, D. (1993). *Ideas For Spelling*. Portsmouth, NH: Heinemann.

Callella, T. (2001). *Making Your Word Wall More Interactive*. Huntington Beach, CA: Creative Teaching Press.

Cambourne, B.L. (1988). *The Whole Story: Natural Learning and the Acquisition of Literacy*. Auckland, New Zealand: Ashton Scholastic.

Clay, M.M. (1991). *Becoming Literate: The Construction of Inner Control*. Portsmouth, NH: Heinemann.

Clay, M.M. (1993). *An Observation Survey of Early Literacy Achievement*. Portsmouth, NH: Heinemann.

Clay, M.M. (1993). *Reading Recovery: A Guidebook For Teachers In Training*. Portsmouth, NH: Heinemann.

Clay, M.M. (2000). *Running Records For Classroom Teachers*. Portsmouth, NH: Heinemann.

Clay, .M.M. (2001). *Change Over Time In Children's Literacy Development*. Portsmouth, NH: Heinemann.

Cowley, J. (1997) *Helping*. Carlsbad, CA: Dominie Press, Inc.

Cunningham, P., and Allington, R. (1994). *Classrooms That Work: They Can All Read and Write*. New York: Longman.

Cunningham, P. (1995). *Phonics They Use*. New York: HarperCollins.

DeFord, D. (2001). *The Dominie Reading & Writing Assessment Portfolio*. Carlsbad, CA: Dominie Press, Inc.

DuFresne, M. (2002). *Word Solvers: Making Sense of Letters and Sounds*. Portsmouth, NH: Heinemann.

Fountas, I., and Pinnell, G.S. (2001). *Guiding Readers and Writers Grades 3-6: Teaching Comprehension, Genre, and Content Literacy*. Portsmouth, NH: Heinemann.

Green, J. (1993). *The Word Wall: Teaching Vocabulary Through Immersion*. Scarborough, Ontario: Pippin Publishing.

Goswami, U., and Bryant, P. (1990). *Phonological Skills and Learning to Read*. Hillsdale, NJ: Lawrence Erlbaum.

Gruber, B. (1999). *How to Use Word Walls*. Cathedral City, CA: Practice & Learn Right Publications.

McCarrier, A., Pinnell, G.S., and Fountas, I. (2000). *Interactive Writing: How Language and Literacy Come Together, K-2*. Portsmouth, NH: Heinemann.

Moustafa, M. (1997). *Beyond Traditional Phonics: Research Discoveries and Reading Instruction*. Portsmouth, NH: Heinemann.

Owens, J. (1992). *One Sock, Two Socks*. Carlsbad, CA: Dominie Press, Inc.

Pinnell, G.S., and Fountas, I. (1998). *Word Matters: Teaching Phonics and Spelling in the Reading/Writing Classroom*. Portsmouth, NH: Heinemann.

Smith, F. (1997). *Reading Without Nonsense*. New York: Teachers College Press.

Swartz, S., Shook, R., Klein, A. et al. (2003). *Guided Reading & Literacy Centers*. Carlsbad, CA: Dominie Press, Inc.

Index